TEACHER'S GUIDE

DAWSON McALLISTER   **TOM MAY**

Copyright © 1986 Shepherd Productions, Inc.

All rights reserved. No part of this book may be reproduced in any form without the permission in writing from the publisher, except in the case of brief quotations embodied in critical articles or reviews.

Verses marked (TLB) are taken from the *The Living Bible,* © 1971 by Tyndale House Publishers, Wheaton, IL. Used by permission.

Verses marked (NIV) are taken from the *Holy Bible: New International Version,* © 1978 by the New York International Bible Society, and are used by permission of Zondervan Bible Publishers.

Verses marked (NKJV) are taken from *The New King James Version.* © 1979, 1980, 1982, Thomas Nelson Inc., Publishers.

Verses marked (NASB) are from the *New American Standard Bible,* © The Lockman Foundation 1960, 1962, 1963, 1968, 1971, 1972, 1973, 1975, 1977.

The use of selected references from various versions of the Bible in this publication does not necessarily imply publisher endorsement of the versions in their entirety.

Printed in the United States of America   ISBN-0-923417-03-6

previously ISBN 0-86606-412-5

Shepherd Ministries
2845 W. Airport Fwy., Suite 137
Irving, Texas 75062
(214)570-7599

CONTENTS

INTRODUCTION

1.	Life Without God	7
2.	Life Without God (cont'd)	13
3.	Life Without Hope	17
4.	Life Without Hope (cont'd)	23
5.	The Big Problem	27
6.	The Real Dilemma	33
7.	Jesus is God	39
8.	Jesus is Man	45
9.	Jesus in the Real World	51
10.	The Cross Makes the Difference	57
11.	Jesus and the Resurrection	63
12.	The Next Move is Yours	69
13.	Review	75

INTRODUCTION

Congratulations! You have one of the highest privileges given to teachers of God's Word — the privilege and responsibility of teaching God's truth to students

You may be a pastor, a Sunday School teacher, a youth pastor, a Christian school teacher, a volunteer youth leader or a parent. But whatever role you're in, God wants to use you in touching students for Him. Can you think of any task more important than helping today's students grasp the solutions to their needs?

Never before have students needed God's answers more than today. Their thoughts and standards are being bombaded constantly by the philosophy and thinking of today's godless society. Every day students are being exposed to humanism, selfishness and hopelessness, with the tragic results evident everywhere.

Youth must know what God says about life if they are to withstand the pressures of the evil that surrounds them. You can be a key person in helping them come to grips with God's answers; you can help students obey God on a day-by-day basis through the power of the Holy Spirit.

No one ever said teaching youth was easy; it is not! They will challenge your resources, question your knowledge and test your faith. But through God's power you can effectively teach youth. It is our prayer that this teacher's guide will help you to be the best communicator that you can be to the youth God brings into your life.

Dawson McAllister and Tom May

USING THE TEACHER'S GUIDE

In order to make your teaching effort more effective, we strongly recommend that each student have his own copy of the discussion manual, "Who Are You Jesus?" Personal involvement in using the manual will produce more discussion, deeper insights and growth by your students.

The discussion manual is essential for teaching from this guide. In fact, without it, this guide is useless, because much of the actual lesson content is contained in it. We urge you to become so familiar with the discussion manual that you can teach from it with confidence.

We recommend that you use your own projects and illustrations with this material. No one knows your students and their circumstances better than you, so be sure to add your personal touch — your creativity and your special gift of teaching. Involve your students in the teaching process — small group and individual projects have been included so that your students can teach themselves. They need to apply these studies to their own immediate life situations, so be ready to supply a personal example that will help them associate the truths you are presenting with a true life situation.

Above all else, emphasize what God says. Scripture is vital in teaching God's truth. You can see that Scripture is highlighted in both the teacher's guide and in the discussion manual. There is a reason for this! Authority comes from the Bible. So does conviction. As you present the eternal Word of God you are giving to your students the resources to change their lives.

LESSON 1
LIFE WITHOUT GOD

> Who Are You, Jesus? is designed to help teenagers recognize that Jesus Christ is the only answer to the problems of cynicism, apathy, hopelessness and despair.

LESSON OBJECTIVE:

Students look down many avenues for meaning and purpose. They seek to find meaning in parents, friends, hard work, partying, money, sex, drugs and alcohol. We do not want them to be deceived with the idea that these endeavors give meaning and purpose to life. The goal of this chapter is to make clear that, in comparison to God, nothing on earth really gives life substance. In this lesson we want to unmask any sense of false security students may have that they can find significance and meaning on their own, apart from God. In love and compassion, we want to lead them to the logical conclusions regarding a life without God.

NOTES FOR PAGE 8 IN STUDENT MANUAL

Have your students turn to the picture on page 8. Begin by asking the question: Why do you think this girl is studying? Or, why do people study? (Be prepared for such answers as, "because they have to" or "to make good grades," but keep on probing and try to help them get beyond the superficial.)

Ask them the following question: Why do the great minds of the world study such things as history, philosophy, science, psychology, and religion? Briefly discuss with them the idea that people study such subjects because they are trying to answer the basic questions of life.

It is important to help your students understand that people study these subjects because they want to find out who we human beings are, in relation to the rest of the world.

Even though in evolution, science has come up with the wrong answers, scientists are trying to find out where man came from.

Historians are also trying to find out what man is like. For example, they study history to see how other periods of time are similar to or different from our day.

High school students need to understand that the key question for the Christian (and the non-Christian) is: Where did I come from? Why am I the way I am? What is ahead for me?

NOTES FOR PAGE 11 IN STUDENT MANUAL

After discussing the picture on page 8, have your students skip page 9 and turn to page 11.

As the teacher, you should be prepared to introduce the list of questions by paraphrasing the first paragraph and then, possibly, sharing a personal example concerning why and how one or more of these questions has been important to you.

Question 1: Ask each student to choose any three questions and in two or more minutes write, on the lines provided, a reason why each of them bothers him. Explain that "bothers" means it is a question that puzzles him or that he wonders about because he is not sure he knows the correct answer.

At the end of the time, ask for several volunteers to share one of the questions they chose and why.

> Special Note To New Teachers: Don't let the deadly silence get to you. Give them plenty of time to think before they start talking. A minute of silence seems like eternity to you, but don't get fidgety. Also, assure them that you are not going to condemn them or make fun of them for whatever answers they give.

NOTES FOR PAGE 12 IN STUDENT MANUAL

As you have your students look at the picture of Solomon on page 12, paraphrase a brief biographical sketch using the information at the bottom of page 11 and the top of page 13. **Question:** How is Solomon like the girl we discussed on page 8? Obviously he is trying to find out the truth about life, just like the girl.

NOTES FOR PAGE 13 IN STUDENT MANUAL

Ask someone in the group to read Ecclesiastes 1:13.

> ***Ecclesiates 1:13 (NIV)***
> *"I devoted myself to study and to explore by wisdom all that is done under heaven."*

Ecclesiastes 1:13 is a statement of Solomon's life purpose.

Clarifying Question: Why do you think Solomon may have devoted himself "to study and to explore by wisdom all that is done under heaven?" You should home in on the idea that Solomon undertook his study in order to determine what life, without God, was like.

Have someone read the paragraph in bold print as well as point "A" of the study.

Next ask someone else to read the two paragraphs that follow.

SOLOMON WANTED TO KNOW WHO MAN REALLY IS

Clarifying Question: What do you think Socrates meant when he said "the unexamined life is not worth living?"

After they have had a few moments to think about that question, you may want to say: "Many Christians talk about the importance of knowing God, but have not struggled with the hard reality of life apart from God."

Question 1: Direct your students' attention to the questions at the bottom of page 13. Ask them to answer this question individually. After several minutes, ask for two volunteers to share what they wrote.

Here is some information that will help you in preparing to deal with these questions: If there is no God, then we are merely a chance collection of atoms. We are on earth as the result of a cosmic accident. Not only are we no different from the other animals, we are actually no different from trees or mountains or anything else. We are no more important; and, in fact, we are worse off because we think we are more important. If there is no God, then our search for meaning and purpose is about as useful as a man gasping for air on the bottom of the ocean.

NOTES FOR PAGE 14 IN STUDENT MANUAL

Have your students focus on the picture on page 15. Ask them: If there is no God what is the difference between the man and the donkey?

If they try to tell you the differences have to do with intelligence and ability, ask them why, if there is no God, it matters which is smarter or more gifted? The obvious answer is that, without God, it really doesn't matter at all.

Have someone read Ecclesiastes 3:18-20 in the box on page 14.

> ***Ecclesiastes 3:18-20 (TLB)***
> *(18) I realized that God is letting the world go on its sinful way so that he can test mankind, and so that men themselves will see that they are no better than beasts. (19) For men and animals both breathe the same air, and both die. So mankind has no real advantage over the beasts; what an absurdity! (20) All go to one place — the dust from which they came and to which they must return.*

Question 1: God wants man to recognize that, without Him, he is just like an animal. God deliberately put man in this position. The despair that comes from honestly admitting he is no different from a frog, for example, sometimes forces a man to reconsider his conclusions.

Question 2: Without God, men and beasts are alike in two ways. They breathe the same air and they die.

Question 3: Men and beasts also share a common form and fate. They both begin as dust, and they both return to the dust. One of the most tragic reminders of the composition of man can be illustrated in the explosion of the space shuttle "Challenger." The interval, from the time the commander of the "Challenger" last communicated with the ground until the time the booster rockets emerged from the explosion, was less than 5 seconds. That means that seven highly trained, remarkably intelligent human beings went from peak functioning efficiency to oblivion in less than 5 seconds.

Question 4: The simple truth is that if man is an accidental product of chance, then it really doesn't matter how he acts. Ultimately, it really doesn't matter how he treats people because all morals are simply a matter of choice. It doesn't matter whether he is cruel or kind, because there is no higher Being (God) who will judge him according to His standards.

Question 5: Allow your students to answer this question without comment from you. Encourage them to be entirely honest.

If you do get the standard youth group answers, pursue the idea that we live on a day-to-day basis what we really believe. Since most teens (even professing Christian teens) often don't live as though God is real, you need to help them understand that it is impossible for them to say they believe in God and act any way they choose.

NOTES FOR PAGE 17 IN STUDENT MANUAL

Have someone read point "B" and the paragraph that follows on page 17.

SOLOMON WANTED TO KNOW IF LIFE ITSELF HAS MEANING

Question 1: Before you discuss it, ask each student to write in his manual the answer to the first question. Then have several students share their answers. This is an opinion question. You should listen carefully to the answers given by your students. This will help you learn where each one is in his thinking.

Next have someone read the line in bold print and the Scripture passage in the middle of page 17.

> *Ecclesiastes 2:13-17 (TLB)*
> *(13) Wisdom is of more value than foolishness, just as light is better than darkness; (14) for the wise man sees, while the fool is blind. And yet I noticed that there was one thing that happened to wise and foolish alike — (15) just as the fool will die, so will I. So of what value is all my wisdom? Then I realized that even wisdom is futile. (16) For the wise and fool both die, and in the days to come both will be long forgotten. (17) So now I hate life because it is all so irrational; all is foolishness, chasing the wind.*

Question 2: The wise man and the fool have two things in common: they both will die and they both will be forgotten soon after their deaths.

Question 3: Far less than 1 percent of the people in the world are remembered very long after their deaths.

NOTES FOR PAGE 18 IN STUDENT MANUAL

Have your students turn to page 18 and examine it for a few seconds. Ask them to mark out the name on the tombstone and replace it with their own name. Next ask them to mark out "FORGOTTEN" on the tombstone, and write down one thing they would like to be remembered for after they have died. Finally ask them, if they were to die right now, would they be remembered the way they would like to be remembered.

NOTES FOR PAGE 19 IN STUDENT MANUAL

Discuss the six questions at the top of page 19.

Question 1: It is a tragedy people are soon forgotten after they die, because it is not the way God intended things to be.

Queston 2: This is another opinion question. Again, allow your students to express themselves without condemnation. Besides needing the freedom to do this, their answers may help you understand them better so that you can more effectively minister to them one-on-one later. At this point, don't try to correct their doctrinal errors or their non-Christian thinking. Use these questions to gain a better understanding concerning where your students are "coming from."

Question 3: Solomon hated life because, without God, it seemed irrational and foolish. To him, life seemed as irrational as a man trying to catch the wind with a butterfly net.

Question 4: Solomon meant by irrational that, without God, life just doesn't make a bit of sense.

Question 5: Solomon meant that trying to find meaning and purpose is useless when you leave God out of your thinking. It would be as easy to catch the wind as it would be to find ultimate purpose in the world without God.

Question 6: This is an opinion question. After they give their opinions, you will want to share the following information with them: If there is no God, then life can never have eternal meaning or significance. No matter how significant a life seems to be while it is being lived, that significance is just an illusion or mirage, since our lifetime is but a fleeting moment in terms of all eternity.

LESSON 2
LIFE WITHOUT GOD
continued

LESSON OBJECTIVE:

The goal is to solidify the thought that without God, mankind has no ultimate purpose or hope for eternal life.

Almost all of your students long for a life that has real purpose. The tragedy is that most people's lives are aimless. This aimlessness is one of the biggest problems facing the American student. Few however trace their aimlessness back to a misunderstanding of spiritual truths. It is also important to know that most students are very concerned about life-after-death. Most assume that eternal life will automatically be there for them. It will be your task to lovingly show them that, apart from the existence of a God they can know, purpose and eternity are, at best, just figments of their imagination.

NOTES FOR PAGE 19 IN STUDENT MANUAL (continued from last lesson)

Review lesson 1 of chapter 1 by reminding your students that we are discovering through King Solomon that a search for answers to life's difficult questions — without God — leads to despair.

Remind them of last week's study where we discovered that without God, man is no different from animals. Solomon came to the conclusion that life without God has no meaning because, like an animal, man dies and its forgotten.

As you begin your new lesson on page 19, ask someone to read point "C" and the two paragraphs at the bottom of page 19.

SOLOMON WANTED TO KNOW IF THERE COULD BE PURPOSE IN A MAN'S LIFE

Then have someone else read Ecclesiastes 2:1.

> ***Ecclesiates 2:1 (TLB)***
> *I said to myself, "Come now, be merry; enjoy yourself to the full." But I found that this, too, was futile, For it is silly to be laughing all the time; what good does it do?*

NOTES FOR PAGE 20 IN STUDENT MANUAL

Have a member of your group read Ecclesiastes 2:20-23.

> ***Ecclesiates 2:20-23 (TLB)***
> *(20) I turned in despair from hard work as the answer to my search for satisfaction. (21) For though I spend my life searching for wisdom, knowledge, and skill, I must leave all of it to someone who hasn't done a day's work in his life; he inherits all my efforts, free of charge. This is not only foolish, but unfair. (22) So what does a man get for all his hard work? (23) Days full of sorrow and grief, and restless, bitter nights. It is all utterly ridiculous.*

Question 1: Soloman decided that enjoying one's self was useless and meaningless. Though pleasure seems alright while it lasts, it fades quickly. After the laughter is over you still have to go home alone and face the reality that you, too, will ultimately die. In the face of death without God, every laugh, smile and pleasure loses its significance.

Question 2: Partying doesn't really help answer the big questions of life. Actually, it causes a person to avoid facing them. Partying is a means of escape from the reality that life seems meaningless and death inevitable. On the surface, partying seems like a lot of fun and it allows a person to avoid the main issues of life!

Question 3: Partying is such a big "turn-on" for people today because of the great amount of meaninglessness and despair in our modern society. Therefore, dulling the pain is an urgent exercise for most people.

Question 4: If the kids in your group are in the norm today, they are involved in a variety of extra-curricular and church activities. Often without thinking about it, students get so involved in day-to-day activities that they do not have time to consider or contemplate the fundamental and most important issues of life. Solomon knew that this type of frenzied activity without time for God led only to "days full of sorrow and grief, and restless, bitter nights."

Question 5: Solomon concluded that, without God, hard work was also meaningless in the end. Hard work means nothing, because it is forgotten in the pain and fear of dying. It doesn't matter how much you have accomplished, or how much money you have earned, the reality of death removes its value. Solomon was frustrated because he realized, in comparison to eternity, his hard work was futile and meaningless.

NOTES FOR PAGE 20 and 23 IN STUDENT MANUAL

Ask someone to read point "D" and the paragraph on pages 20 and 23.

SOLOMON ALSO WANTED TO KNOW IF THERE IS LIFE AFTER DEATH

NOTES FOR PAGE 23 IN STUDENT MANUAL

Next have someone else read Ecclesiastes 9:4-6.

> ***Ecclesiates 9:4-6 (TLB)***
> *(4) There is hope only for the living. "It is better to be a live dog than a dead lion!" (5) For the living at least know that they will die! But the dead know nothing; they don't even have their memories. (6) Whatever they did in their lifetimes — loving, hating, envying — is long gone, and they have no part in anything here on earth any more.*

Question 1: Ecclesiastes 9:4-6 gives a small ray of hope for those living without God. At least the living know that they will die. Life gives them the opportunity to reflect on their mortality and turn to God. To paraphrase Solomon in Ecclesiastes 7:2, "It is better to spend your time in a funeral home, than at a party since every man is destined to die."

Question 2: Solomon saw death as a terrible thing because everything that a man does during this life is gone when he dies. Dead men have nothing to do with life on earth after they are dead.

Question 3: This is an opinion question, so allow your students to express themselves freely. After you have heard different student's opinions you may want to add to them. Actually, there are many reasons people are afraid to die. Some are afraid to die because of the unknown — they aren't sure what is on the other side of death. Others are afraid to die because they do not want to leave "loved ones" who are still here. Others are afraid to die because they are relatively sure what lies on the other side and they know they are not prepared for it.

Question 4: This is also an opinion question. Depending on where he is spiritually, each student will have a somewhat different opinion. If we look at death through the eyes of man without God, it is easy to conclude that the same fate befalls all creatures. Through temporal eyes, the death of a human being seems no more significant than the death of a house pet.

Conclude this lesson on an upbeat note. Encourage your young people to understand that this lesson on life and death is designed to help them see the importance of seeking to know the way to eternal life.

Have someone read Ecclesiastes 12:1.

> ***Ecclesiates 12:1 (TLB)***
> *Don't let the excitement of being young cause you to forget about your Creator. Honor him in your youth before the evil years come — when you'll no longer enjoy living.*

Solomon's point is that many, indeed most, youth think that being young is an opportunity to party, have a good time and do their own thing. They have fooled themselves into believing they will have plenty of time later to think on eternal issues. Solomon says in Ecclesiastes 12:4-7, "... man goes to his eternal home and mourners go about the streets. Remember Him (God) — before the silver cord is severed, or the golden bowl is broken; before the pitcher is shattered at the spring; or the wheel broken at the well, and the dust returns to the ground it came from, and the spirit returns to God who gave it." (NIV)

Solomon concluded the book of Ecclesiastes with these words, "Now all has been heard; here is the conclusion of the matter: Fear God and keep His commandments, for this is the whole duty of man. For God will bring every deed into judgment, including every hidden thing, whether it is good or evil (Ec 12:13-14 NIV).

The purpose of the following lessons is to help students get to know the true God so that they can learn to fear Him and keep His commandments.

LESSON 3

LIFE WITHOUT HOPE

LESSON OBJECTIVE:

The purpose of this lesson is to help students understand that, apart from God, there are only two alternatives to the curse of meaninglessness. They are despair and escapism.

NOTES FOR PAGE 25 IN STUDENT MANUAL

Begin by dividing your youth into small groups of four or five students. Have each group appoint a spokesperson. Ask them to discuss these questions: Is it possible for someone who does not know God to have hopes and dreams? Why or why not? If you think that it is possible for a person who does not believe in God to have hopes and dreams, what kinds of hopes and dreams might they have?

After your students have discussed this for a few minutes, gather together in one group. Have each spokesperson make a report of their conclusions to the whole group.

Then ask the group the following important question: How may a Christian's hopes and dreams be different from the hopes and dreams of a non-Christian? The answer to this question should be an adequate review of the first two lessons.

Now, ask someone to read the first paragraph of chapter 1, page 25. Have your students turn to the scripture references which follow the first question. Ask them to list the things Solomon tried in his quest for reality and satisfaction. Also ask them to answer the other two questions on this page.

Question 1: In Ecclesiastes 1:17 we see that Solomon sought to understand wisdom, madness and folly. As Solomon looked around he saw some men acting wisely while other men acted foolishly and without thinking. To compound the situation, he also noted that some men lived in madness or despair. This verse really gives an outline of chapter 2. In this chapter we will be looking at the three alternatives available to modern man.

DESPAIR THAT LEADS TO SELF-DESTRUCTION

The first alternative is despair. This is what Solomon called madness. Madness or despair result when a person concludes that life is absolutely pointless and meaningless.

The second alternative is escapism. Solomon called this folly. Folly is simply trying to answer eternal longings for purpose and meaning with temporal or materialistic acquisitions.

The third alternative is wisdom. Wisdom is the search to know God. It is based on a belief that life is rational and meaningful because there is a rational, loving Creator at the foundation of everything.

In Ecclesiastes 2:1-10 we see that Solomon tried pleasure in his search for satisfaction. When that didn't work, he tried hard work. In his hard work, he acquired much property and he became very wealthy. Solomon even says, in Ecclesiastes 2:9, that he became greater than anyone before him.

Question 2: While your students may come up with several specific activities which Solomon did not try, they cannot come up with any new *categories*. Solomon tried every category available to man: wisdom, madness, foolishness, pleasure, work, wealth, and fame. There are no other categories.

Question 3: Solomon concluded by saying in Ecclesiastes 2:10-11, "I denied myself nothing my eyes desired; I refused my heart no pleasure. My heart took delight in all my work, and this was the reward for all my labor. Yet when I surveyed all that my hands had done and what I had toiled to achieve, everything was meaningless, a chasing after the wind; nothing was gained under the sun." (NIV)

After explaining these truths to your students, help them see Solomon's frustrations through their teenage eyes.

Ask someone to read point "A" on page 25 and the first paragraph.

NOTES FOR PAGE 26 IN STUDENT MANUAL

Have your students look at the picture of the guy holding the gun on page 27. Ask them to explain why they think someone might decide to kill himself. What kind of pressures or situations could cause a person to decide that life is not worth living, or that it is meaningless?

Next, you should read the poem on page 26 to your students. [Read this poem aloud several times before you try to read it to your students. The better you are able to read it, the greater the impact will be.] Another suggestion is that you might ask one of your better readers to practice beforehand and read it aloud to the group. For the poem to be highly effective, choose a student who is interested in drama or debate.

Question 1: Discuss with the group the question at the bottom of page 26. Your students will tell you that the boy killed himself because his family life was bad, or because Father Tracy died, or because he just felt like nobody cared. Help them to see that this is not the total reason. Due to the work of secular psychologists and psychiatrists, we have falsely concluded that people commit suicide because the circumstances of life go bad (and certainly they contribute to the problem). But the simple truth is that many people live relatively normal happy lives in spite of the fact that they have experienced similar hardships.

The real issue is that many people have concluded that life is not worth living, because they believe that life is without meaning or purpose. Having decided this and then having experienced "bad times," they ultimately conclude that living is futile and decide to end their own life.

NOTES FOR PAGE 28 IN STUDENT MANUAL

Discuss the questions on page 28.

Questions 1 and 2: Perhaps his mother, father, sister, Father Tracy or the professor could have each helped him some, but we have no evidence from this poem that they didn't try. We also know that his mother and father were unhappy due to the fact that their marriage was not a good one. The only one in the poem who could really have helped him was God, but he apparently didn't look for God or get past "religion," because the poem says, ". . . and he forgot how the end of the 'Apostles Creed' went . . . "

On page 28, you will find a second poem dealing with despair and suicide. Again, you should practice this poem before you read it to your group. [Poetry is designed to be read aloud. Generally, its effectiveness will be lost when read silently.]

NOTES FOR PAGE 30 IN STUDENT MANUAL

As a group, discuss the questions on page 30.

Question 1: Several things happened that led the girl in the poem to despair. She decided that life was meaningless and without purpose. Apparently she was unwilling to see how God could use these problems in her life to strengthen her character. Instead, she yielded to bitterness and despair because she had lost her mother and her friends. To make matters worse she took an escapist attitude by turning to liquor. This compounded her situation. Because she had experienced some difficult times, she gave up on trusting anyone. In looking at the last verse — "people will try to stop; they'll tell me that they care. But I know I won't believe them for lies are everywhere" — it seems that she deliberately decided that she would not trust anyone else.

Question 2: It seems that both of these young people decided that life was not only painful; it was also meaningless. They just gave up!

Have someone read the paragraph after the second question.

Question 3: This is an opinion question. It is designed to cause teens to think about despair and its symptoms. By thinking of someone whom they think experiences despair, they should be able to isolate certain symptoms that illustrate the problem. Apathy and depression are two of the symptoms.

Question 4: This question is a much tougher question for teens to answer because it is so personal. Unless you have an extremely open and responsive group, it may be a little hard for them to open up and admit their feelings. Perhaps you can help the situation by sharing a time when you experienced despair. Try to be honest and vulnerable about the pain you felt. Be careful not to try and gloss over your pain with spiritual platitudes. Teens need to understand that trusting God does not minimize the pains of being human in a fallen world; it simply gives us hope in spite of the pain.

ESCAPISM THAT IGNORES REALITY

Have someone in your group read point "B" and the following paragraph.

NOTES FOR PAGE 31 IN STUDENT MANUAL

Ask one of your students to read aloud the Scripture passage on page 31.

> **Luke 12:16-21 (TLB)**
> *(18) A rich man had a fertile farm that produced fine crops. (17) In fact, his barns were full to overflowing — he couldn't get everything in. He thought about his problem, (18) and finally exclaimed, 'I know — I'll tear down my barns and build bigger ones! Then I'll have room enough. (19) And I'll sit back and say to myself, "Friend, you have enough stored away for years to come. Now take it easy! Wine, women, and song for you!"'*
> *(20) But God said to him, 'Fool! Tonight you die. Then who will get it all?'*
> *(21) Yes, every man is a fool who gets rich on earth but not in heaven.*

Ask your students why we would call the rich man in this story an escapist. How was he avoiding reality? You might also want to quiz them regarding the rightness or wrongness of acquiring possessions.

The point of this parable is not that it is wrong to own things or be wealthy, but that this man thought he was in control of his life. He thought that he could take care of himself with material possessions, while excluding God from the process. As a result, when he died, he had nothing.

NOTES FOR PAGE 32 IN STUDENT MANUAL

Discuss the three questions at the top of page 32.

Question 1: Using the Scripture passage on page 31 as the basis, we know that God considers the escapist a fool.

Question 2: An escapist is called a fool because he tries to avoid ultimate issues by filling his life with superficial or temporal solutions.

Question 3: The list is endless. Some people pursue wealth and fame through athletics, while others pursue it through business or professions. Others are less concerned with the material results of working hard; instead, they simply seek satisfaction through the work itself. The benefits of wealth and fame are merely ways of marking success for others to see. Still other people escape the despair of their empty lives by turning to mind-altering chemicals such as beer, wine, cocaine and other drugs.

LESSON 4
LIFE WITHOUT HOPE
continued

LESSON OBJECTIVE:

The goal of this lesson is to help students understand that only a genuine search for God will supply meaning and purpose for a person's life.

Begin this lesson by briefly reviewing the main points of the last discussion. Have them thumb through their notes on pages 25-32 and tell you what they learned from the last lesson.

NOTES FOR PAGE 32 IN STUDENT MANUAL (continued from last lesson)

SEARCH FOR GOD THAT SUPPLIES PURPOSE

Ask someone to read point "C", the first paragraph and Proverbs 14:13. Then discuss the question at the bottom of page 32.

> *Proverbs 14:13 (TLB)*
> *Laughter cannot mask a heavy heart. When the laughter ends, the grief remains.*

Question 3: In regard to that question, many teens try to deal with their despair and sense of hopelessness by making jokes. Johnny Rivers, a popular singer from the '60's, sang a song called "The Tracks of My Tears." In it he said, "People say I'm the life of the party 'cause I tell a joke or two. Although I may be laughing loud and hearty, deep inside I'm blue. So take a good look at my face, you'll see my smile looks out of place. In the closeup, it's easy to trace: The tracks of my tears."

Ask your students what they think Pascal meant when he said man had a "God-shaped" hole in his soul. Basically, Pascal meant that God has created us in such a way that we will never be satisfied with life until we allow him to become the main feature and overriding desire of our lives.

Using the idea that without God we are like bubbles "floating on a sea of infinity," point out to your students that the life expectancy of a bubble floating in the ocean is absurdly short. It is even more discouraging when you realize that, no matter how pretty the bubble was, after it pops, it just becomes water in the ocean again. Using this analogy, it should be easy for anyone to see that, if there is no God, then man is utterly doomed to insignificance and unimportance.

NOTES FOR PAGE 33 IN STUDENT MANUAL

Have one of your students read the lyrics of the song by Les Hughey.

> *Saturday mornin', sleepin' in till noon*
> *Same old weekend, same old room*
> *What a great party, at least that's what I was told*
> *But if it's so great, then why does it seem so old*
>
> *I know there's got to be something more*
> *More than I've been livin' for*
> *Right now I feel I'm missin' the real game*
> *I need to change, I need to change*
>
> *Look at the night sky, please explain why*
> *Is there a reason, do we just live and die*
> *Why do I feel empty, why do I feel wrong*
> *I've had all the answers, but they don't last long*
>
> *I know there's got to be something more*
> *More than I've been livin' for*
> *Right now I feel I'm missin' the real game*
> *I need to change, I need to change*
>
> *"Something More" Les Hughey*
used by permission

Ask the first question found on page 35. The main force motivating the person in the song to seek more meaning in life was his "gut feeling" that there was more to life than he was experiencing.

Next, have someone else read the paragraph and the Scripture passage that follows the song.

> **Psalm 63:1 (TLB)**
> *Oh God, my God! How I search for you! How I thirst for you in this parched and weary land where there is no water. How I long to find you!*

This Scripture passage is extremely important. It actually sets the stage for the rest of our study. Using this verse as the basis, it is important for you to help each student, no matter where he is spiritually, to realize that as long as he is on this planet, God wants him to be a seeker.

NOTES FOR PAGE 35 IN STUDENT MANUAL

Spend a few minutes discussing the second and third questions at the top of page 35.

Question 4 and 5: These are important questions. At this point, you must allow the different students in your group to be honest. Don't become intimidated by students who express philosophies of despair or escapism. Instead, commend them for their honesty. Don't push them to accept Christian answers, but encourage them to honestly investigate them.

Using the box in the center of the page as a basis, end this part of the lesson by emphasizing that it doesn't really matter which of the three responses they have been following until now. God has promised to reveal the truth to people who have a sincere desire to know God and find answers to some of the difficult questions of life.

In the middle of page 35 in bold print is a "FIT GOD INTO A 'HARD ANSWERS' PROJECT." Read the instructions to your group. Encourage them to look back over their notes on chapters 1 and 2 to get their answers. Then ask each student to answer by himself the two scenarios at the bottom of page 35 and the one scenario at the top of page 37.

After they have had a few minutes to complete their answers, ask several students to share their responses.

Your students probably are going to come up with very spiritual-sounding "religious" answers. As you discuss their answers, *IT IS IMPORTANT* to help them to see that these first two chapters have not given spiritual answers. Instead, these first two chapters have pointed out that, if there is no God, there is really no reason to continue living. Up to this point, we have only alluded to spiritual solutions. Basically, if a person believes in God but knows no more than is included in the first two chapters, there is nothing substantive he can tell another person that will stop him from wanting to end his life. The first two chapters have been designed to clarify the issues, not to give solutions to them.

NOTES FOR PAGE 37 IN STUDENT MANUAL

Conclude this lesson by reading the last two paragraphs and the Scripture passage on page 37.

> ***Ecclesiastes 3:20-21 (NIV)***
> *All go to the same place; all come from dust, and to dust all return. Who knows if the spirit of man rises upward and if the spirit of the animal goes down into the earth?*

Man, created in the image of God and ruined by the fall, still has an inner consciousness that God exists and must be reckoned with in some way. The last eight chapters of this book will show you how to know God and live eternally.

LESSON 5

THE BIG PROBLEM

LESSON OBJECTIVE:

The purpose of this chapter is to help students consider that, while mankind has an innate belief in a Supreme Being, most men are living in rebellion against God.

NOTES FOR PAGE 39 IN STUDENT MANUAL

Break into groups of three or four and discuss the four questions listed on page 39. Encourage the students to express their views freely.

Bring everybody back together after a few minutes and ask several people to share their answers with the whole group.

Below is a brief look at each individual question, and some possible responses.

Question 1: This is purely an opinion question.

Question 2: To say that there are "no atheists in foxholes," basically means that everyone prays when they think they are about to die. Many people, who throughout their lives have confessed atheism or agnosticism, find themselves praying when life gets really tough.

Question 3: Again, this is an opportunity for your kids to do the talking. You should sit back and listen for a few minutes and be available to clarify any questions they might have.

Question 4: This is also an opinion question. Treat it in the same manner as the one above. This may be an opportunity to give your opinions, if no one in the group is talking much.

After the discussion, you should briefly summarize the four points we are going to study in depth in this lesson:

    a. Man is God-conscious.

    b. Man does not live a life that pleases God.

    c. Man has turned away from God.

    d. Man suppresses the truth about God.

MAN IS GOD-CONSCIOUS

Have someone read the bold print, point "A", and the first paragraph at the bottom of page 39 and the top of page 40.

NOTES FOR PAGE 40 IN STUDENT MANUAL

Ask someone else to read the bold print and the Bible verse at the top of page 40. Discuss the first question.

> ***Romans 1:19 (TLB)***
> *For the truth about God is known to them (mankind) instinctively;*
> *God has put this knowledge in their hearts.*

Question 1: Romans 1:19 states that God has put the knowledge of who He is deep in the soul and mind of every person. This knowledge of God is so real that no man can completely erase it. Now ask someone to read the paragraph that follows the question. It gives further clarification to this question.

Question 2: This is another open-ended question. It is designed to help each person remember when they first realized that God existed. If you can get a person to take this question seriously, it will force even the most hardened atheist or agnostic to admit that, at least early in life, he believed in the existence of God.

Ask someone in the group to read the bold print and the paragraph at the bottom of page 40. Then discuss the question at the bottom of the page.

Question 3: After you have gotten the opinions of several students in the group, point out that there is really only one good explanation for man's desire to worship: God put it there.

NOTES FOR PAGE 42 IN STUDENT MANUAL

Have someone read the bold print and the Scripture verse on page 42. Then discuss the two questions related to this area.

> ***Romans 1:20 (TLB)***
> *Since earliest times men have seen the earth and sky and all God made, and have known of his existence and great eternal power.*

You may have to explain what the word "tangible" (in the caption) means. Basically, it refers to something you can see, feel, taste, touch or hear. In this case, we mean that God has given us evidence we can objectively study regarding whether or not He exists.

Question 1: God has given us much evidence in nature for His existence. Ask your students to think of evidence from nature they believe gives validity to the idea that God exists. The natural evidence for the existence of God is almost inexhaustible.

Question 2: According to Romans 1:20, if a person ponders or meditates on God's creation, he can find out that God exists and that He has eternal power. Ask your students for some evidence in nature that God has eternal power.

Have someone read the next paragraph aloud.

Question 3: Ask each person to take a few minutes to answer the question at the bottom of page 42. Insist that each person turn in his Bible to Job 38 in order to find his answers.

NOTES FOR PAGE 44 IN STUDENT MANUAL

Ask someone in the group to read Psalm 19:1 at the top of page 44. Then ask each one to read the paragraph under the Bible verse.

> ***Psalm 19:1 (TLB)***
> *The Heavens are telling the glory of God; they are a marvelous display of his craftsmanship.*

Question 1: Have your group do the exercise of writing a prayer to God.

After your group has had a few minutes to compose their prayers, ask them to bow their heads. Suggest that several pray their prayers to God as they read them from their workbooks.

MAN DOES NOT LIVE A LIFE THAT PLEASES GOD

The second point of this lesson poses the problem that exists between God and man. Your students need to understand that, while men and women everywhere believe in the existence of God, it does not change the fact that many do not have a desire to please God or to know Him.

Summarize point "B" and the information under this point. Use Jeremiah 29:13 to show that God wants to make Himself known to people who truly desire to know Him.

> *Jeremiah 29:13 (NASB)*
> *And you will seek Me and find Me, when you search for Me with all your heart.*

Question 2: Discuss the question at the bottom of the page. Answers to this will vary, but it would be wise to remind your students of the truths they learned in the first few lessons about despair and escapism.

NOTES FOR PAGE 46 IN STUDENT MANUAL

Summarize or have someone read aloud the material at the top of the page. Discuss the first question.

> *Romans 3:10-11 (TLB)*
> *No one is good — no one in all the world is innocent. No one has ever really followed God's paths, or even truly wanted to.*

Question 1: According to Romans 3:10-11, there is no one who has ever truly sought to follow God because, as the picture on page 47 says, "We are rebel's at heart."

MAN HAS TURNED AWAY FROM GOD

Ask someone to read point "C" and the Bible verse.

> *Romans 3:12 (TLB)*
> *Every one has turned away; all have gone wrong. No one anywhere has kept on doing what is right; not one.*

Question 2: Ask each person to individually work the exercise at the bottom of the page. [Tell your students that this is *NOT* something you will ask them to discuss. This exercise is just for their own personal benefit.]

NOTES FOR PAGE 48 IN STUDENT MANUAL

MAN SUPPRESSES THE TRUTH ABOUT GOD

Read point "D" and Romans 1:18.

> ***Romans 1:18 (TLB)***
> *But God shows his anger from heaven against all sinful, evil men who push away the truth from them.*

Question 1: Illustrate this answer by asking your students how many of them have ever taken cough medicine when they were sick with a cold. What was the purpose of the medicine? Obviously it was to stop or suppress the cough. People do the same thing with God in their minds and consciences. They deliberately try to block out the truth about God. One way that people suppress the truth of God is by denying that He even exists.

Question 2: In the middle of the page is a Bible exercise to help your students see some different ways people suppress the truth about God. Have them work this exercise on their own.

Psalm 14:1 teaches that some men suppress the truth about God by denying that He exists. God calls a person like that a fool.

Psalm 50:20-21 teaches that other men suppress the truth of God by dealing in hatred toward another person. This is a form of suppressing God's truth because God has told us to love and care for each other. Anytime we fail to obey God's commandments we are guilty of suppressing the truth of God by the very way we live.

Isaiah 29:15-16 shows that man tries to suppress the truth of God by lying to himself and saying that God doesn't really see or understand the evil he is about to do.

In John 3:12, Jesus made it very clear that people who do not want to know the truth about earthly things certainly can not understand the truth about heavenly things. Many people look to natural phenomena (the theory of evolution is an example) for explanations which will exclude God. They do this because they are suppressing the truth about God.

In John 3:19, people also suppress the truth of God because they do not want to know how bad they are. Rather than face up to the fact that they are sinful, rebellious and depraved, they hide behind excuses. They look for all kinds of ways to explain why their actions are not really as bad as they appear.

Conclude this lesson by answering the question at the bottom of the page regarding Romans 1:18.

Question 3: God responds to people who suppress the truth with anger. Many people want to believe that God is only a God of love. The Bible teaches that God uses His wrath and anger to judge sin and evil.

Read or summarize the paragraph at the bottom of page 48.

LESSON 6
THE REAL DILEMMA

LESSON OBJECTIVE:

The purpose of this chapter is to help your students understand that since God cannot and will not change Himself or His laws, we must change.

NOTES FOR PAGE 49 IN STUDENT MANUAL

In the last chapter we looked at the problem of man's rebellion against God and his suppression of the truth. Although technically, because God is God, He never has a problem, this chapter examines the apparent dilemma that existed between the holiness of God, the justice of God and the love of God. Since man had sinned against God, how was He to exercise and maintain His holiness, justice and love perfectly? To simply overlook man's sin and rebellion would have been to compromise His holiness and justice. To have punished man without providing him with any way to escape judgment would have been to compromise the love of God.

Have someone read the first paragraph on page 49. Emphasize that God can in no way change — He always remains the same.

From here, you should move in the lesson to the idea expressed in the bold print — GOD HAS A PLAN FOR MAN. Emphasize that before a person can properly understand God's plan for man, he needs to understand a little bit about the character of God. In this chapter we will briefly examine several aspects of His character — His holiness, justice, and love.

GOD IS INFINITELY HOLY

Have someone in the group read point "A". Ask them to individually answer the question following point "A".

Question 1: After allowing the class to struggle with this difficult spiritual definition, have each member individually read the second paragraph from the bottom of the page. Using that definition, ask them to go back and fill in the previous question.

You should go on to explain that the word "holy" means "to be set apart." In other words, when we say that God is holy, we mean that He is set apart from the rest of His Creation; there is nothing and no one else like Him. Actually, we can take each of the characteristics of God and add the word "holy" before it. For example, God is holy merciful (His mercy is different and set apart from every other kind of mercy); God is holy loving (His love is perfect and incomparable when measured against human love); God is holy forgiving (His forgiveness is unlike anyone else's forgiveness in all the world).

NOTES FOR PAGE 50 IN STUDENT MANUAL

Read 1 Samuel 2:2.

> *1 Samuel 2:2 (NKJV)*
> *There is none holy like the Lord, for there is none besides You, nor*
> *is there any rock like our God.*

NOTE: You might substitute the words "set apart" in every verse that speaks of the holiness of God.

Allow them to spend a few seconds answering the two questions on this page.

Question 1: According to 1 Samuel 2:2, we know that God is so holy that He is not like anyone or anything.

Question 2: As they share their description of the holiest person they have ever known, ask them what made this person seem to be holy. Ask them what kinds of things this person did or didn't do. Your aim is to help them see that this person is, in many respects, set apart (or different) from the other people they know.

Read the last two paragraphs and the Scripture passage in the box on the bottom half of the page.

> *Psalm 111:9 (NKJV)*
> *He has sent redemption to His people;*
> *He has commanded His covenant forever:*
> *Holy and awesome is His name.*

NOTES FOR PAGE 53 IN STUDENT MANUAL

Ask the first question on this page.

Question 1: Any God who was perfectly holy would be awesome. He would not be like anything else.

Have someone read the paragraph after the first question and the two Scripture passages that follow.

> ***Isaiah 6:3 (NKJV)***
> *"Holy, holy, holy, is the Lord of hosts;*
> *The whole earth is full of His glory!"*

> ***Isaiah 6:5 (NKJV)***
> *"Woe is me, for I am undone!*
> *Because I am a man of unclean lips,*
> *And I dwell in the midst of a people of unclean lips;*
> *For my eyes have seen the King, The Lord of hosts."*

Discuss the two questions at the bottom of the page.

Question 2: The angels were worshiping God. To say that He is holy is the highest word of praise a created being can say to God. It communicated a recognition of the fact that God is not like anything that is created.

Question 3: Isaiah reacted to God's holiness in the way he did because he was struck by his own impurity as he came face-to-face with the ultra purity of God. In the light of God's holiness, Isaiah recognized how terribly sinful he was. It brought him to his knees in fear and trembling.

NOTES FOR PAGE 55 IN STUDENT MANUAL

Have someone read the text (including the Bible verse) at the top of the page.

> ***Habakkuk 1:13 (NIV)***
> *Your eyes are too pure to look on evil, you cannot tolerate wrong.*

Questions 1 and 2: Have your students break into groups of three or four, and do the exercise in the middle of the page.

Have someone read the text in the middle of the page (above point "B").

GOD IS ABSOLUTELY JUST

Then have someone else read point "B" and the Bible verse.

> **Psalm 11:7 (NIV)**
> *For the Lord is righteous, he loves justice; upright men will see his face.*

NOTES FOR PAGE 57 IN STUDENT MANUAL

Allow your students a few minutes to answer the two questions at the top of the page.

Question 1: Psalm 11:7 teaches us that God loves justice.

Question 2: To say that God is just is to say that He is fair. God has a holy, just standard and He judges all men according to that standard. God does not show partiality. All men, no matter who they are, will be judged by the absolutely perfect and fair Law of God.

Have someone read the text (including the Bible verse).

> **Psalm 96:13 (NIV)**
> *They will sing before the Lord, for he comes, he comes to judge the earth. He will judge the world in righteousness and the peoples in his truth.*

NOTES FOR PAGE 58 IN STUDENT MANUAL

Have someone read the Bible verse at the top of the page. Then discuss the question.

> **Psalm 11:7 (NIV)**
> *For the Lord is righteous, he loves justice; upright men will see his face.*

Question 1: Psalm 96:13 teaches us that God will someday come to judge the earth. His standard for determining His judgments will be righteousness and truth. In other words, God will take each man and compare his individual life to the standards of God's Word. He won't make up a different standard for each man. Instead, He will judge each man completely and fairly. Psalm 11:7 adds that only upright men (men who have done everything right) will see His face.

Read the paragraph in the center of the page. Have each of your students read Psalm 139:1-4 and answer the questions.

Question 2: According to Psalm 139:1-4, God knows everything about us. He knows when we sit down and when we stand up. He knows what we are going to say before we say it. He even knows all our thoughts.

Question 3: This is an opinion question. Students in rebellion against God will not like the fact that He knows everything about them. The student who desires to know God will be very glad that He cares enough to know about Him.

Read the Bible verse and text at the bottom of the page.

> *Jeremiah 17:10 (NIV)*
> *I the Lord search the heart and examine the mind, to reward a man according to his conduct, according to what his deeds deserve.*

NOTES FOR PAGE 59 IN STUDENT MANUAL

Read the paragraph at the top of the page.

Before you begin this next section, ask your students this question: If God were only holy and just, what do you think would be the fate of man? The obvious answer is that God would frown upon all men. Because of His perfect justice and His desire to uphold the right, God's only choice would be to judge man and destroy him utterly.

GOD IS TOTAL LOVE

Have someone read the text beginning with "THE LOVE OF GOD." After they read the text, discuss the questions at the bottom of the page.

> *1 John 4:16 (NIV)*
> *"And so we know and rely on the love God has for us. God is love. Whoever lives in love lives in God, and God in him."*

Question 1: When we turn to God, it is His love that we rely on.

Question 2: We can know what love is because God is love. This means that as we get to know God through faithfully reading His Word, we will come to an increasingly better understanding of what love is.

Question 3: The statement that God is love means that God is the essence of love. If you understand who He is and why He acts the way He does, then you will understand what love is. All of God's actions are based upon love, His special love for His creation.

NOTES FOR PAGE 61 IN STUDENT MANUAL

Have someone read the text at the top of page 61. Then discuss the questions at the bottom of the page.

> ***Jeremiah 31:3 (NIV)***
> *The Lord appeared to us in the past, saying: "I have loved you with an everlasting love; I have drawn you with loving-kindness."*

Question 1: Everlasting love is love that never ends. It is true that God never enjoys punishing members of His creation. God loves everyone! His amazing love for His creation is unconditional. No one falls outside the realm of His love.

Question 2: Lovingkindness is God's active response to man. The greatest example of God's lovingkindness was the gift of His Son for the sin of mankind.

Question 3: God is behind every act of true love, even when non-Christians are involved.

Question 4: All genuine love is a gift from God. If God were not the source, then man would be incapable of love.

NOTES FOR PAGE 63 IN STUDENT MANUAL

Have someone read the text on page 63. You may want to conclude this study by emphasizing the first sentence of the second paragraph which says, "It would appear at first glance that God also had His own challenge."

Of course the truth is that God has never had a challenge or a problem in the sense that we have. Because God is God and He knows everything — past, present and future — He has always known that His creation would be sinful and He has always known how He would handle the problem.

LESSON 7
JESUS IS GOD

LESSON OBJECTIVE:

The purpose of this chapter is to help students clearly see that Jesus Christ was not just a moral teacher or great religious leader; He was God in the flesh.

NOTES FOR PAGE 65 IN STUDENT MANUAL

Begin the meeting by asking the whole group this question: In your opinion, who was Jesus Christ? Allow a few minutes for comment.

Have someone read the first paragraph. Then discuss the question.

Question 1: Remind your group that God is holy and just. Help them to see that the only possible punishment God could have considered for their disobedience and evil ways was eternal separation from His presence.

Have someone read the bold print and the paragraph underneath it. Focus on the idea that Jesus was not just a great man or a moral teacher. In fact, He was God coming in a body of flesh to rescue man from drowning in a situation in which he could not save himself.

THE BIBLE TELLS US THAT JESUS IS GOD

Have someone read the bold print, point "A", and the paragraph at the bottom of the page.

NOTES FOR PAGE 66 IN STUDENT MANUAL

Ask your group to turn in their Bibles to John 1:1-14 (or provide them with copies). Have someone read this passage.

> ***John 1:1-2 (NASB)***
> *In the beginning was the Word, and the Word was with God and the Word was God. He was in the beginning with God.*

You want to emphasize verse 14 which makes it clear that "the Word" spoken of in verses 1-2 was Jesus.

Have someone read the verse in the box at the top of page 66, then discuss the four questions relating to Jesus as the Word.

Question 1: Jesus is called the Word. Since He is God, He is the perfect expression of who God is. Personality is a characteristic of God. One of the foremost marks of genuine personality is the desire and ability to communicate. God has always possessed the perfect ability to communicate the truth about Himself.

Summarize or have someone read the paragraph underneath the first question.

Question 2: The four facts we learn about Jesus in John 1:1-2 are:
- He was in the beginning.
- He was with God.
- He was God.
- He was with God in the beginning.

Question 3: This question is self-explanatory.

Question 4: We find that these verses teach that Jesus was not just with God; He was God.

JESUS CLAIMED TO BE GOD

Have someone read point "B" and the paragraph at the bottom of the page.

NOTES FOR PAGES 68 AND 69 IN STUDENT MANUAL

Have someone read the Scripture passage and the paragraph at the top of the page. Then discuss the four questions.

> ### John 14:7-9 (NASB)
> *(7) "If you had known Me, you would have known My Father also; from now on you know Him, and have seen Him." (8) Philip said to Him, "Lord, show us the Father, and it is enough for us." (9) Jesus said to him, "Have I been so long with you, and yet you have not come to know Me, Philip? He who has seen Me has seen the Father; how do you say, 'Show us the Father'?"*

Question 1: Seeing or knowing the Father is the basic need of all people because God has created us to both know and love Him.

Question 2: Jesus is saying that if men have seen and heard Him, then they have seen and heard the Father. Jesus is the physical representation of God to man.

Question 3: No mere man could make this statement about himself because it would simply be too arrogant. Jesus was the only one who could make this statement because He was God in the flesh.

Question 4: If what Christ said about Himself is true, then when we read and study about Jesus, we can be sure that we are also gaining an understanding of the Father.

JESUS ALLOWED OTHERS TO CLAIM AND WORSHIP HIM AS GOD

Summarize or have someone read the text at the bottom of page 68 and the top of page 69.

> ### John 5:18 (NASB)
> *For this cause therefore the Jews were seeking all the more to kill Him, because He not only was breaking the Sabbath, but also was calling God His own Father, making Himself equal with God.*

NOTES FOR PAGE 70 IN STUDENT MANUAL

Discuss the questions on page 70.

Question 1: Even Jesus' enemies recognized that He was claiming to be God. Those people who say that Jesus did not claim to be God have not read the Bible very closely. Even His enemies understood what He was claiming.

Question 2: The second question is definitely related to the first one. Jesus' enemies clearly understood that He was claiming to be God.

Question 3: No mere man could be equal with God. In order to be equal with God, a person must be God. Since men are not God, then it is impossible for them to be equal with Him.

Question 4: Jesus was either equal with God or He was lying. If He was lying, then He could not have been a great teacher or a good man, because He was a liar. On the other hand, if He was not a liar, then His words are true and He is certainly more than a great teacher or a good man.

Question 5: At no point in the gospel accounts do we find Jesus trying to convince His enemies that He was equal with God. He did not have to do this because He was God.

Summarize the paragraph below the questions and have someone read the Scripture passage.

> *John 20:26-29 (NASB)*
> *(26) And after eight days again His disciples were inside, and Thomas with them. Jesus came, the doors having been shut, and stood in their midst, and said, "Peace be with you." (27) Then He said to Thomas, "Reach here your finger, and see My hands; and reach here your hand, and put it into My side; and be not unbelieving, but believing." (28) Thomas answered and said to Him, "My Lord and my God!" (29) Jesus said to him, "Because you have seen Me, have you believed? Blessed are they who did not see, and yet believed."*

NOTES FOR PAGE 72 IN STUDENT MANUAL

Discuss the questions on page 72.

Question 1: After Thomas had seen the resurrected Christ, he fell on his knees and said, "My Lord and my God!"

Question 2: Thomas was not exaggerating when he called Jesus God. He knew that men do not rise from the dead. In Thomas' mind there was only one explanation: Jesus was God.

Question 3: Jesus did not correct Thomas for calling Him God, because Jesus is God.

Question 4. Jesus told Thomas that those who were truly blessed were those who believed in Him without having seen Him in His risen state.

Question 5. You are fortunate if you believe in Jesus, because it means that you have examined the evidence that Jesus is God and you have decided that it is true. On that basis, you have put your faith in Jesus Christ as your Savior and Lord.

Read or summarize the paragraph after question 5.

Discuss question 6.

Question 6: These are things Jesus did that only God could do:

- Mark 2:5-11 — He forgave sins.
- Matthew 25:31-34 — Jesus taught that one day He will sit on His throne and judge all the peoples of the world.
- Colossians 1:16-17 — These verses teach that Jesus created all things, that He was before all things, and that by Him all things hold together.

Have someone read the bold print, the paragraph and the Scripture verse at the bottom of page 72.

> *John 1:14 (NASB)*
> *And the Word became flesh, and dwelt among us, and we beheld His glory, glory as of the only begotten from the Father, full of grace and truth.*

NOTES FOR PAGE 74 IN STUDENT MANUAL

Have someone read the paragraph at the top of page 74.

Question 1: As you close this session, have your students write out a personal prayer of thanks to Jesus for what He means to them. After they have had a few minutes, ask them to bow their heads. Encourage those who will to read their prayer aloud.

LESSON 8
JESUS IS MAN

LESSON OBJECTIVE:

The purpose of this chapter is to help students clearly see that Jesus Christ was not only God, but that He was also fully human.

NOTES FOR PAGE 77 IN STUDENT MANUAL

Before your students open their books you should ask the following question: "Who was Jesus Christ?" After the last lesson, they should be able to tell you a great deal about His deity. When they have finished sharing their insights, have them turn to page 77 in the workbook. Explain that Jesus is God, but that He was also fully man.

JESUS IS MORE THAN GOD

Have someone read or you should summarize the text on page 77. Be sure to have someone read aloud the Scripture passage at the bottom of the page.

> *Matthew 8:23-27 (NASB)*
> *(23) And when He got into the boat, His disciples followed Him. (24) And behold, there arose a great storm in the sea, so that the boat was covered with the waves; but He Himself was asleep. (25) And they came to Him, and awoke Him, saying, "Save us, Lord; we are perishing!" (26) And He said to them, "Why are you timid, you men of little faith?" Then He arose, and rebuked the winds and the sea; and it became perfectly calm. (27) And the men marveled, saying, "What kind of man is this, that even the winds and the sea obey Him?"*

45

NOTES FOR PAGE 78 IN STUDENT MANUAL

Discuss the six questions at the top of page 78.

Question 1: According to Matthew 8:24, Jesus was sleeping.

Question 2: There are several reasons why Jesus would be asleep at a time like this. First of all, he was apparently tired and needed the rest. He also must have known that He was in a safe environment and that His life was not in danger. Because Jesus believed His Heavenly Father and trusted God's plan for His life and the life of His disciples, He knew that they were not about to die. Therefore, He was able to sleep in the midst of a storm, while all those around Him (who were probably as tired as He) were terrified.

Question 3: While Scripture teaches that God neither sleeps nor slumbers, we must recognize that Jesus was fully man and therefore had the capacity to become tired.

Question 4: Jesus demonstrated the fact that He is God in Matthew 8:26 when He calmed the storm with His words. No one but God has control over the weather. Even modern man with his multitude of inventions is not able to alter weather patterns. As a matter of fact, even with all these scientific instruments, we don't do a very good job of predicting the weather!

Question 5: In Matthew 8:27, Jesus' disciples called Him a man. They recognized that He was completely human. They knew He needed sleep and they knew He ate food as they did. In other words, being completely human, Jesus had the same body functions that we do.

Question 6: The big question these men were asking about Jesus was not, "Is He a man?" Instead, they were asking: "What kind of man is this?" It was obvious to them that He was a man. It was also obvious to them that He was something more than a man.

JESUS IS FULLY HUMAN

You should summarize or have someone read the text at the bottom of page 78.

NOTES FOR PAGE 80 IN STUDENT MANUAL

Have someone read the text on page 80.

Hebrews 4:15 (NKJV)
For we do not have a High Priest who cannot sympathize with our weaknesses, but was in all points tempted as we are, yet without sin.

NOTES FOR PAGE 81 IN STUDENT MANUAL

Discuss the three questions at the top of page 81.

Question 1: Jesus can sympathize with our weaknesses because He was tempted in every way we are tempted. Even for Jesus, fighting temptation was not without struggle. For example, in the Garden of Gathsemane, just prior to His crucifixion, He was tempted to choose another path. Apparently the struggle was so intense that the Scriptures tell us He sweat real blood.

Question 2: Even though Jesus was sinless, He experienced many of the same struggles that we experience, such as exhaustion, fear, hunger, loneliness and pain. Because of this, Jesus can still sympathize with our human sufferings.

Question 3: Jesus, while not lured by temptation and sin, felt the full force of that power and destructiveness. Therefore, He sympathizes and hurts with us when we fall into the trap of sin.

Have your students break into groups of three or four. Each group should do the project at the bottom of page 81. After a few minutes, ask each group to share with the whole group the insights they have gained.

Question 4: Here are some answers your students may give. The list should not be considered exhaustive. If they come up with one that is not on the list, be careful about deciding that Christ did not experience it.

- I get tired; so did Christ.
- I get hungry; so did Christ.
- I get thirsty; so did Christ.
- I get sleepy; so did Christ.
- I get lonely; so did Christ at the Cross.
- I get fearful; so did Christ at the Cross.
- I get angry; so did Christ.
- I get frustrated; so did Christ.
- I feel happiness; so did Christ.
- I feel joy; so did Christ.

- I have a need for the sense of belonging; so did Christ.
- I experience love; so did Christ.
- I get sad; so did Christ.
- I feel guilt; so did Christ on the Cross.
- I feel confused; so did Christ on the Cross.
- I feel depressed; so did Christ.
- I get excited; so did Christ.
- I have friends who mistreat or misunderstand me; so did Christ.

Question 5: Jesus felt the physical pangs of hunger, thirst and weariness that all human beings experience. He also felt the emotions that all human beings experience.

NOTES FOR PAGE 82 and 83 IN STUDENT MANUAL

JESUS IS A GREAT MYSTERY

Have someone read the text on these two pages.

> ***Romans 11:33 (NKJV)***
> *Oh, the depth of the riches both of the wisdom and knowledge of God! How unsearchable are His judgments and His ways past finding out!*

NOTES FOR PAGE 84 IN STUDENT MANUAL

Summarize or have someone read the text on page 84.

> ***Romans 11:34 (NKJV)***
> *For who has known the mind of the Lord? Or who has become His counselor?*

Discuss the question at the bottom of the page.

Question 1: A poem entitled "Compression" may help to answer this question:

Compression by Tom May

Too tight jeans,

and a seam-bursting "T-shirt"

Minutely remind me of how

You must have felt.

The God of All,

Creator of the vast universe;

Author of black holes,

And supernovas;

Organizer of constellations,

And galaxies,

And solar systems.

Crammed

Into a baby's body.

Enduring limitation

And suffering;

Suddenly unable to be

All places at once.

The King of Heaven;

From absolute mobility

To relative paralysis.

A baby,

A servant,

A casualty.

For what reason?

Can the mystery be so simple as to call it

"Unconditional Love"?

Summarize or have someone read the last paragraph at the bottom of page 84.

NOTES FOR PAGE 86 IN STUDENT MANUAL

JESUS BECAME MAN TO DEAL WITH OUR REBELLION AGAINST GOD

Summarize or have someone read the text on page 86.

> ***Hebrews 2:14-17 (TLB)***
> *(14) Since we, God's children, are human beings — made of flesh and blood — he became flesh and blood too by being born in human form; for only as a human being could he die and in dying break the power of the devil who had the power of death. (15) Only in that way could he deliver those who through fear of death have been living all their lives as slaves to constant dread. (16) We all know he did not come as an angel but as a human being — yes, a Jew. (17) And it was necessary for Jesus to be like us, his brothers, so that he could be our merciful and faithful High Priest before God, a Priest who would be both merciful to us and faithful to God in dealing with the sins of the people.*

Have each individual student do a mini Bible study on Hebrews 2:14-17. If possible, allow them about 10 minutes for this.

Here is a list from Hebrews 2:14-17 of the things that Jesus did and is doing for us by becoming a man:

- He became flesh and blood like us.
- He came to die as we do.
- His death broke the power of the devil and death over us.
- He gave mankind, who fears death, the opportunity to be freed from fear.
- He is our merciful and faithful High Priest before God.
- He was made like us in every way.
- He satisfied God for our sins.

Conclude this lesson by having each student write a prayer of thanksgiving to Christ.

LESSON **9**

JESUS IN THE REAL WORLD

LESSON OBJECTIVE:

The purpose of this chapter is to help students clearly see that Jesus Christ was not an unapproachable God in a human body, but rather a very real person, an understanding human being who came to earth in order to allow men and women to know God.

NOTES FOR PAGE 89 IN STUDENT MANUAL

Before you have your students turn to page 89, ask them to describe Jesus Christ during His earthly life. This should serve to remind them of the things they learned in the previous lessons. This should also serve to help you spot any misconceptions they may have developed.

JESUS WAS THE GREATEST TEACHER IN HISTORY

Summarize or have someone read the top half of this page. Be sure to have someone read the Scripture verses in the box on page 89.

> *Matthew 9:35-36 (NASB)*
> *And Jesus was going about all the cities and the villages, teaching in their synagogues, and proclaiming the gospel of the kingdom, and healing every kind of disease and every kind of sickness. And seeing the multitudes, He felt compassion for them, because they were distressed and downcast like sheep without a shepherd.*

Then discuss the question at the bottom of the page.

Question 1: Regarding the question, Jesus did so much teaching because the people were ignorant of the truth. They had many religious teachers, but most were simply teaching their own ideas rather than the truth from God. One of the things Jesus did while He was here on earth was to correct much of the false religious teaching the people had received.

NOTES FOR PAGE 91 IN STUDENT MANUAL

Summarize or have someone read the text at the top of the page. Then divide your group into smaller groups of 2 or 3. Have them complete the exercise in the middle of the page. This passage, Matthew 7:7-11, is an excellent passage for them to see several methods Jesus used to teach His followers.

> ***Matthew 7:7-11 (TLB)***
> *(7) Ask, and you will be given what you ask for. Seek, and you will find. Knock, and the door will be opened. (8) For everyone who asks, receives. Anyone who seeks, finds. If only you will knock, the door will open. (9) If a child asks his father for a loaf of bread, will he be given a stone instead? (10) If he asks for fish, will he be given a poisonous snake? Of course not! (11) And if you hardhearted, sinful men know how to give good gifts to your children, won't your Father in heaven even more certainly give good gifts to those who ask him for them?*

Question 1: Jesus used *timely repetition* in His teaching. In other words, he repeated an idea several times so the people would remember it. In this case, He repeats the idea of "asking, seeking and knocking" twice at the very beginning of this teaching. Then, in slightly different words, He repeats Himself as He illustrates it and applies it.

Jesus *meaningfully illustrated* His teaching with stories or ideas we can picture in our minds. Who cannot visualize in his mind a child asking for a loaf of bread and his father giving him a stone; or a child asking for a fish and receiving a poisonous snake instead?

Jesus clearly makes a *practical application* of this teaching to the people. They cannot misunderstand what He is saying when He declares that, if they who are sinful know how to take care of their children, certainly God who is not sinful knows how to provide good gifts for His earthly children.

We also see in this passage that Jesus has a very *concise conclusion.* In one sentence Jesus makes His point. Most teachers and preachers use hundreds of words and dozens of sentences to make a point. Instead, Jesus uses the fewest words possible to make His point clear. Using as few words as possible is one mark of an excellent teacher.

Summarize (or have someone read) the text at the bottom of the page. Then discuss the question at the bottom.

> ***Matthew 7:28-29 (NASB)***
> *The result was that when Jesus had finished these words, the multitudes were amazed at His teaching; for He was teaching them as one having authority, and not as their scribes.*

Question 2: Of course, Jesus' secret to being a great teacher was that He spoke with authority.

NOTES FOR PAGE 93 IN STUDENT MANUAL

Discuss the question at the top of the page.

Question 1: Jesus got His authority from God the Father. In Matthew 28:18, Jesus said, "All authority in heaven and on earth has been given to me." (NKJV) The implication in this verse is that God the Father had given Jesus all authority. His authority came from God.

Have someone read the text and scripture beneath the first question. Then discuss the two questions that follow.

> ***Matthew 24:35 (NASB)***
> *"Heaven and earth will pass away, but My words shall not pass away."*

Question 2: Christ's teachings are important to us because, like God Himself, they are eternal and unchangeable. In a world of constantly changing moral and ethical values, mankind needs a standard by which to judge right and wrong. Christ's teachings provide us with that solid standard.

Question 3: This is an opinion question.

Summarize or have someone read point "B" and the text following. Then discuss the question that follows.

Question 4: There is certainly more than one reason why it was necessary for Jesus to model the Christian life for us. First, God wanted to demonstrate through Jesus that the Christian life could be lived. Jesus set the standard for living the Christian life. He did not just come to give us a cold set of rules to follow. He came to show us that a relationship with God was both possible and rewarding. While it is true that He gave us His written Word, it is even more fantastic to realize that He came and lived on planet earth as the Living Word. That is to say, He lived out on planet earth the standard which He has set for us.

JESUS IS THE GREATEST MODEL OF HOW TO PLEASE GOD

Summarize or have someone read the last paragraph on page 93.

NOTES FOR PAGE 95 IN STUDENT MANUAL

First have someone read the Scripture passage in the box at the top of the page. Summarize the paragraph that follows. Then discuss the question.

> ***John 13:5 (NKJV)***
> *After that, He poured water into a basin and began to wash the disciples' feet, and to wipe them with the towel with which He was girded.*

Question 1: Washing someone else's feet would be a humbling experience today. In Jesus' day it was even more humbling because the roads were hot and dusty and the people could not stay as clean as the people do today. It must have been a very grimy job to wash the feet of eleven men who had spent a hot day walking long dusty roads.

Read the text and Scripture passage in the bottom half of the page. Then discuss the question at the bottom of page 95.

> ***John 13:12-17 (TLB)***
> *(12) After washing their feet he put on his robe again and sat down and asked, "Do you understand what I was doing? (13) You call me 'Master' and 'Lord,' and you do well to say it, for it is true. (14) And since I, the Lord and Teacher, have washed your feet, you ought to wash each other's feet. (15) I have given you an example to follow: do as I have done to you. (16) How true it is that a servant is not greater than his master. Nor is the messenger more important than the one who sends him. (17) You know these things — now do them! That is the path of blessing."*

Question 2: Jesus was trying to teach His disciples the importance of demonstrating their love for each other by becoming servants to each other. Jesus wanted these people to understand that genuine love is evidenced by how we treat one another.

NOTES FOR PAGE 96 IN STUDENT MANUAL

Discuss the questions at the top of the page.

Question 1: We should never think that we are too good to do acts of loving service because Jesus was not above doing them. Certainly if He, as God, was willing and capable of doing them, how can we say that we are too good to do them. After all, He is the King of all Creation.

Question 2: The second question is primarily an opinion question.

Summarize the text beneath the two questions and explain the project to your group.

Question 3: This is an individual activity. As your students are doing this activity, give them time to think about their answer before writing it down.

JESUS SUFFERED WHEN HE LIVED ON EARTH

Have someone read point "C" and the text following it.

> ***Isaiah 53:3 (NKJV)***
> *A man of sorrows and acquainted with grief.*

Discuss the question at the bottom of page 96.

Question 4: Because Jesus was without sin, He experienced more suffering than other people because He was aware of what life was supposed to be like. As He walked around seeing the suffering and pain that people experienced, it grieved (and hurt) Him because He knew that this was not the way He had intended life to be when He created the world.

NOTES FOR PAGE 99 IN STUDENT MANUAL

Summarize the text at the top of the page and read the Scripture in the box. Then discuss the two questions.

> ***2 Peter 2:7-8 (NKJV)***
> *And delivered righteous Lot, who was oppressed with the filthy conduct of the wicked. For that righteous man, dwelling among them, tormented his righteous soul from day to day by seeing and hearing their lawless deeds.*

Queston 1: 2 Peter 2:7-8 teaches us that Lot experienced a great deal of mental and spiritual anguish as he daily witnessed sin and its effects in the world around him.

Question 2: Certainly Jesus, because of His sinlessness, experienced a great deal more pain and anguish over the sins of the world than Lot did.

Summarize or have someone read the two paragraphs at the bottom of the page.

NOTES FOR PAGE 100 IN STUDENT MANUAL

This last page is not one that you should read through quickly. As a teacher, you should be prepared to close this lesson with this Scripture, talking from the heart on what Christ endured in coming to earth.

> ***Isaiah 53:3-5 (TLB)***
> *(3) We despised him and rejected him — a man of sorrows, acquainted with bitterest grief. We turned our backs on him and looked the other way when he went by. He was despised and we didn't care. (4) Yet it was our grief he bore, our sorrows that weighed him down. And we thought his troubles were a punishment from God, for his own sins! (5) But he was wounded and bruised for our sins. He was chastised that we might have peace; he was lashed — and we were healed!*

NOTE: The conclusion of this lesson sets up the last three lessons of this study. We will focus on the Crucifixion, the Resurrection, and, finally, your students personal response to the message.

Lesson 10
THE CROSS MAKES A DIFFERENCE

LESSON OBJECTIVE:

The purpose of this chapter is to help students understand that the death of Jesus Christ was no accident. Instead, it was an integral part of God's plan for redeeming sinful man.

NOTES FOR PAGE 103 IN STUDENT MANUAL

Summarize or have someone read the first paragraph. Read together in unison the Scripture verse in the box. Then discuss the question that follows it.

> *Luke 13:32-33 (NIV)*
> *Go tell that fox, 'I will drive out demons and heal people today and tomorrow, and on the third day I will reach my goal.' In any case, I must keep going today and tomorrow and the next day — for surely no prophet can die outside Jerusalem!*

Question 1: Jesus was saying that the primary goal of His life was to die. Many people try to escape or avoid the idea that the main reason Jesus came to earth was to die. They say that His primary reason for coming to earth was to teach men how to live and respect each other. While He did do that, He repeatedly said that His main purpose in coming to earth was to die for the sins of the world.

CHRIST BECAME A MAN TO DIE

Summarize or have someone read the text at the bottom of page 103 and the top of page 104.

NOTES FOR PAGE 104 IN STUDENT MANUAL

Have someone read the Scripture passage in the box at the top of page 104. Then discuss the two questions beneath it.

> ### John 12:27 (NKJV)
> *"Now My soul is troubled, and what shall I say? 'Father, save Me from this hour'? But for this purpose I came to this hour."*

Question 1: A "troubled soul" makes you feel heavy inside. A knot seems to grow inside your chest or stomach and it seems as though you can't keep going. It becomes hard to think clearly because your emotions try to overrule your mind.

Question 2: When Jesus spoke of "this hour," He was speaking of the hour in which He was to die. He didn't literally mean an exact 60 minutes. Instead, "this hour" is a symbolic term meaning "this time," this particular moment in history.

Have someone read the text beneath the two questions. Then discuss the two questions at the bottom of page 104.

> ### Matthew 20:28 (NIV)
> *The Son of Man did not come to be served, but to serve, and give his life a ransom for many.*

Question 3: Jesus served people all during His earthly life. He healed the sick and fed the multitudes who came to hear Him preach and teach.

Question 4: When Jesus said that He came "to give His life a ransom for many," He meant that He was going to sacrifice His sinless life for the lives of all who had sinned.

NOTES FOR PAGE 106 IN STUDENT MANUAL

CHRIST BECAME A MAN TO TAKE OUR BURDENS

Summarize the text and read the Scripture passage at the top of this page. Then discuss the two questions that follow.

> ### Hebrews 5:7 (NKJV)
> *Who, in the days of His flesh, when He had offered up prayers and supplications, with vehement cries and tears to Him who was able to save Him from death, and was heard because of His godly fear.*

Question 1: Undoubtedly, the most difficult part of facing the Cross was not the pain of dying. Instead, it was the fact that He would have to take upon Himself the sins of the world. For One so spotless and pure, the thought of dirtying Himself with sin, which He had never known, was excruciatingly painful.

Question 2: This second question goes back to our study of the character of God in chapter 4. Because of the holiness and justice of God, it was impossible for man to enter into God's presence covered with sins. Yet, because of His love for man, God wanted to provide a way for man to enter His presence. The only way God could satisfy His holiness and justice, and still allow man the opportunity to come into His presence, was for Christ to take man's sins upon Himself and suffer God's punishment for sin.

Have someone read the text at the bottom of the page.

> *Hebrews 12:2 (NASB)*
> *Fixing our eyes on Jesus, the author and perfecter of faith, who for the joy set before Him endured the cross, despising the shame, and has sat down at the right hand of the throne of God.*

NOTES FOR PAGE 107 IN STUDENT MANUAL

Discuss the questions at the top of the page.

Question 1: Jesus endured the shame of the cross so that sinful man might be given the opportunity to be cleansed from his sins and enter into the presence of God.

Question 2: The "joy set before Him" means that He also saw it as a great privilege to stand in man's place and receive man's punishment. There was divine satisfaction in correcting man's disobedience in the Garden of Eden. More than anything in all creation, God wanted to redeem the fallen race. For Him it was worth the greatest sacrifice of all — His very own Son.

CHRIST BECAME A MAN TO PAY FOR OUR SINS

Summarize, then have someone read the text in the middle section of page 107. Discuss the two questions at the bottom of the page.

> *John 3:17 (NKJV)*
> *For God did not send His Son into the world to condemn the world, but that the world through Him might be saved.*

Question 3: Jesus did not come to condemn the world. The truth of the matter is that, because of sin, the world was already condemned. Man, through his sin, brought condemnation on himself. Jesus did not come to pronounce a final word of condemnation upon man. Instead, He came so that through His death, He could "uncondemn" man.

Question 4: The Bible says that believing in Jesus is the only way a person can receive forgiveness and come into a right relationship with God. Acts 4:12, speaking of Jesus, says, "Salvation is found in no one else, for there is no other name under heaven given to men by which we must be save" (NIV). It is through Jesus Christ alone that man is saved to eternal life.

NOTES FOR PAGE 109 IN STUDENT MANUAL

Summarize the text at the top of the page, then have someone read the Scripture passage. Discuss the question in the middle of the page.

> ### Isaiah 53:5-6 (NKJV)
> *"But He was wounded for our transgression, He was bruised for our iniquities; The chastisement for our peace was upon Him, And by His stripes we are healed. All we like sheep have gone astray; We have turned, every one, to his own way; And the Lord has laid on Him the iniquity of us all."*

Question 1: When Christ was crucified, He was not just wounded physically. During His death, He took upon Himself the sins of mankind. In this way, He who had known no sin, experienced the painfully oppressive weight and power of sin and its judgment.

Divide into small groups of two or three. Have each group work together to complete the project at the bottom of page 109 and the top of page 111.

- God has given man food; man has twisted it into glutony.
- God has given man a desire for rest; man has twisted it into laziness.
- God has given man sleep; man has twisted it into a way to avoid reality.
- God has given man creativity; man has twisted it into finding new ways to do evil.
- God has given man power to take care of the world; man has twisted it to rape and destroy nature.
- God has given man sex; man has twisted it into lust.

NOTES FOR PAGE 111 IN STUDENT MANUAL

The first section of this page is a continuation of the project begun on the previous page.

- God has given man His love; man has twisted it into the idea that God doesn't care what he does.

- God has given man His holiness; man has twisted it into the idea that God cannot be pleased.

- God has given man a desire to have a good time to encourage him; man has twisted it into a "let's party all the time" attitude that destroys him.

- God has given man patience; man has twisted it into the idea that he will never be judged by God.

- God has given man justice; man has twisted it into the idea that all men ought to have equal amounts of money, property and education.

Discuss the question immediately following the project.

Question 1: Isaiah is also teaching us that it was only because of Christ's death that we are able to be healed of our sins. He declares that we were spiritually sick and in need of a doctor. Jesus, through His death, provided the only medicine strong enough to kill the deadly power of sin.

Summarize the text in the middle of the page, and have someone read the Scripture passage from Isaiah. Then discuss the question at the bottom of page 111.

> *Isaiah 53:6 (NKJV)*
> *And the Lord has laid on Him (Jesus) the iniquity of us all.*

Question 2: Christ must have suffered greatly to have all the sins of the world laid upon Him. Sin is an oppressive burden. It separates us from understanding and enjoying the love and fellowship of our Heavenly Father. Jesus Christ had intimately and perfectly known that love and fellowship. There had been no time in His life when He was not in perfect fellowship with His Father. Suddenly to be cut off must have been an awful experience. It is no wonder that He shouted out, "My God, my God, why have you forsaken me?"

NOTES FOR PAGE 112 IN STUDENT MANUAL

Have someone read the text (including the Scripture passage) at the top of this page. Then discuss the questions at the bottom of the page.

1 John 4:9-10 (TLB)
God showed how much he loved us by sending his only Son into this wicked world to bring to us eternal life through his death. In this act we see what real love is: it is not our love for God, but his love for us when he sent his Son to satisfy God's anger against our sins.

Question 1: In 1 John 4:9-10 we see several ways God proved that He loved us through the crucifixion of Jesus Christ. First, the very act of sending His Son proved that He loves us. Second, He allowed that same Son to be put to death in order that man might be forgiven of his sins. Third, God did not wait until we fell in love with Him before He took care of the problem. In reality, He took care of the problem before we were ever born; even before we knew we had a problem.

Question 2: Teachers, on this last question, allow your students several minutes to work on their own. Your students need to come to grips with the idea that Jesus has taken away all of their reasons for living in despair.

LESSON 11
JESUS AND THE RESURRECTION

LESSON OBJECTIVE:

The purpose of this chapter is to help your students realize that, if Jesus Christ was not raised from the dead, Christianity is useless. While in reality the Crucifixion and Resurrection of Jesus Christ cannot be separated from each other, your students need to understand the importance of the Resurrection as expressly validating the deity of Christ.

NOTES FOR PAGE 117 IN STUDENT MANUAL

CHRIST'S RESURRECTION PROVES THAT HE IS GOD

Summarize the text at the beginning of the chapter and then discuss the question.

Question 1: It has been correctly stated that Christianity stands or falls on the Resurrection. If Jesus did not rise from the dead then Christianity is no better than any other religion. As a matter of fact, if Christ did not rise from the dead, Christianity is worse than any other religion. After all, no other major religious leader claimed to be God. Jesus, alone, made this claim. If His claim was false, then He does not deserve the respect He holds in the religions of the world. The Resurrection stands as the measuring stick for the validity of Christianity.

Summarize the text at the bottom of the page.

NOTES FOR PAGE 118 IN STUDENT MANUAL

Have someone read the Bible passage at the top of the page. Then discuss the question underneath it.

> **Matthew 16:21 (NIV)**
> *From that time on Jesus began to explain to his disciples that he must go to Jerusalem and suffer many things at the hands of the elders, chief priest and teachers of the law, and that he must be killed and on the third day be raised to life.*

Question 1: As you can see from this passage, Jesus not only predicted that He would die, He also predicted that He would rise again from the dead. If the resurrection did not occur we must conclude that either Jesus deliberately lied to His disciples, or that He was ignorantly deluded into thinking that He was God and that He was going to rise again from the dead. If He was a blatant liar or an insane man, we neither owe Him respect nor should we desire to be like Him. Only a fool would want to commit himself to follow a deceiver and fraud.

Summarize or have someone read the text and the Scripture passage beneath the first question. Then discuss the question beneath it.

> **Acts 2:24 (NIV)**
> *God raised him from the dead, freeing him from the agony of death, because it was impossible for death to keep its hold on him.*

Question 2: It was impossible for death to hold Jesus Christ because He was God. As God, He had defeated sin. Sin is what caused death to enter the world in the first place. If that which brought death into the world was defeated by Christ, then death itself was no longer able to hold Christ in the grave. It had no power over Him and He was free to rise from the dead.

Summarize the text at the bottom of the page.

NOTES FOR PAGE 120 IN STUDENT MANUAL

Read the passage at the top of this page. Then summarize the text beneath it.

> **Romans 1:4 (TLB)**
> *By being raised from the dead he was proved to be the mighty Son of God, with the holy nature of God himself.*

This next section deals with the fact that, since Christ was true to His word about rising from the dead, we can also trust Him to fulfill those portions of His Word which have not yet taken place. Certainly, if He could rise from the dead, He is capable of completing all that He said He would do.

Question 1: Have each student work individually to determine what else Christ has promised He will do.

- John 14:1-3 teaches us that Jesus Christ has gone to prepare a place for all those who follow Him, and that He is coming back one day to take them to that place.

- 1 John 3:2 teaches us that when Christ comes back, He will make all His followers to be perfect like Him. In other words, we will all become like Christ.

- In Matthew 25:31-34 we learn that when Christ returns, all the people of all the nations will come before Him to be judged. He will separate the people of the world into two groups — those who have believed and followed Him, and those who have not believed in Him and lived in disobedience.

Question 2: The question at the end of this exercise is an opinion question. It should help you discover where your students need to grow in their faith in Christ.

CHRIST'S RESURRECTION PROVIDES NEW HOPE

Summarize or have someone read the text at the bottom of page 120.

NOTES FOR PAGE 122 IN STUDENT MANUAL

Have someone read the Scripture passage at the top of the page.

> ***Romans 6:23 (NKJV)***
> *The wages of sin is death, but the gift of God is eternal life in Christ Jesus our Lord.*

Question 1: Although physical death is one result of sin, death in Romans 3:23 does not refer only to physical death. It is also referring to spiritual death. The simple fact is that we are all born spiritually dead. This is why Jesus told the woman at the well in John 4 that she must be "born again."

Question 2: Death is a curse because it keeps us from being what we were created to be — people in fellowship and harmony with God. Nothing could be worse then to build something and never use it for what it was designed to do. Man is very much the same. He was created to know, love and serve God. He spends his whole life trying to fill his life with "things" that will make him happy, while the only thing that will really make him happy is knowing, loving and serving God.

Have someone read the text and Scripture verses at the bottom of page 122.

> ***Romans 6:9 (NKJV)***
> *Knowing that Christ, having been raised from the dead, dies no more. Death no longer has dominion over Him.*
>
> ***John 11:25-26 (NKJV)***
> *I am the resurrection and the life. He who believes in Me, though he may die, he shall live. And whoever lives and believes in Me shall never die. Do you believe this?*

NOTES FOR PAGE 124 IN STUDENT MANUAL

Discuss the two questions at the top of the page.

Question 1: When Jesus called Himself "the Resurrection and the Life," He meant that He alone was able to give men new life. This is what He said in John 14:6: "I am the way and the truth and the life. No one comes to the Father except through me."

Question 2: When Jesus said that if we believe, "we may die but *yet* we will live," He was saying that He will ultimately come and raise us from the dead. Jesus has promised that He will raise to eternal life all Christians who have died. A Christian does not need to fear death. Due to the Resurrection of Jesus Christ, he can have great confidence in the fact that he, too, will be raised from the dead.

CHRIST'S RESURRECTION MEANS HE CAN HELP US

Read or summarize the paragraph on prayer and discuss its implications.

CHRIST'S POWER IS ALWAYS AVAILABLE

Ask someone to read Matthew 28:20 and explain how this promise applies to our daily lives.

> ***Matthew 28:20 (NASB)***
> *Lo, I am with you always, even to the end of the age.*

NOTES FOR PAGE 127 IN STUDENT MANUAL

Have someone read the Scripture passage at the top of the page. Then discuss the questions that follow.

> ***Philippians 3:10 (NIV)***
> *I want to know Christ and the power of his resurrection and the fellowship of sharing in his sufferings, becoming like him in his death.*

Question 1: We can know the power of Christ's resurrection by trusting in Him. As God, He alone is able to meet our needs and give us the power to live obedient Christian lives.

Question 2: Christ's resurrection power can become a reality in our lives. As we learn to look to Christ for power and knowledge, He will, through His Word, show us what it means to obey and how to be obedient. The most important element in experiencing Christ's resurrection power is desiring to obey Him. In John 14:21, Jesus said, "Whoever has my commands and obeys them, he is the one who loves me. He who loves me will be loved by my Father, and I too will love him and show myself to him" (NIV).

Question 3: The simple fact is that few people experience Christ's power in their lives because they do not truly desire to obey Him.

Question 4: This question is designed to cause your students to think seriously about their relationship with Christ. If you lead an average group, most of them will have to admit, if they are honest, that they really don't have the relationship with Christ which they desire. Encourage them to share with you the things in their lives that make them think that they cannot live a powerful Christian life. Even as they share these things with you and the group, encourage them to believe that Christ hears them and will strengthen them in His power. Also stress that living a powerful Christian life is a matter of growth. It is a process that takes place in a person's life as they get to know Christ better each day and continues over a period of many months and years. They can live in Christ's power today, even though imperfectly!

NOTES FOR PAGE 128 IN STUDENT MANUAL

Conclude this lesson by summarizing or adding to the conclusion.

> ***1 Corinthians 15: 14, 17, 19 (NIV)***
>
> *(14) And if Christ has not been raised, our preaching is useless and so is your faith.*
>
> *(17) And if Christ has not been raised, your faith is futile; you are still in your sins.*
>
> *(19) If only for this life we have hope in Christ, we are to be pitied more than all men.*

If you have a personal story or illustration that would help this lesson come alive for your students, share it!

Lesson 12
THE NEXT MOVE IS YOURS

LESSON OBJECTIVE:

The purpose of this chapter is to help students realize that they must make their own decision about Jesus Christ. They need to recognize that Christianity is not just something to do on Sunday. Following Christ is something to do all the time.

NOTES FOR PAGE 131 IN STUDENT MANUAL

Summarize the text on page 131. Teacher, this is a very important lesson in which you will encourage your students to make a commitment to Jesus Christ. Therefore, you should be able to speak from your heart using the material on this page. Spend much time reading and preparing the material for this lesson. It also stands to reason that you cannot communicate this lesson without much prayer.

BEING RELATED TO GOD REQUIRES BELIEVING IN CHRIST

NOTES FOR PAGE 132 IN STUDENT MANUAL

Discuss the two questions at the top of the page.

Question 1: Many people fail to take a close look at Jesus Christ because they are turned off by the people who claim to be His followers. Many people who claim to be followers of Jesus Christ do not maintain an open and responsive attitude toward Christ. As a result, non-Christians refuse to respond to Christ. They simply do not see professing Christians taking Him seriously.

Question 2: There are a number of tough questions one must ask before becoming a Christian. Among them are: How can I be sure that Jesus Christ is really God? What does commitment to Christ mean on a practical day-by-day level? Am I really ready to reject my old way of life and commit myself to following Christ no matter where He may lead?

Summarize or read the text, read the Bible verse and discuss the two questions.

> *John 7:17 (NIV)*
> *If anyone chooses to do God's will, he will find out whether my teaching comes from God or whether I speak on my own.*

Question 3: According to John 7:17 a person must be willing to do God's will before he will know whether Christ's teachings are true or not.

Question 4: There is one basic attitude a person must have in order to show that he "chooses to do God's will." He must desire to know the truth and to follow the truth no matter what it costs.

Have someone read the text and the Bible verse at the bottom of the page.

> *Jeremiah 29:13 (NKJV)*
> *And you will seek Me and find Me, when you search for Me with all your heart.*

NOTES FOR PAGE 133 IN STUDENT MANUAL

Have someone read the text at the top of the page, then discuss the question.

Question 1: This is an opinion question. Since most people are not willing to be completely open to knowing God, this may be a rather prying question. Don't avoid it! If nothing else, your students need to come to grips with the fact that they have not been completely honest with themselves about their relationship to God.

BEING RELATED TO GOD
REQUIRES ADMITTING OUR SIN

Have someone read point "B" on page 133.

NOTES FOR PAGE 134 IN STUDENT MANUAL

Summarize or have someone read the text at the top of page 134. Then discuss the question.

Question 1: Some of the rationalizations people use to keep from admitting they have a sin problem are:

- I'm not a really bad person.
- I'm no worse than anyone else.
- It's the devil's fault I did wrong.
- I just don't have any self-control.
- Everybody does it.
- God isn't that strict anyway.

Summarize or have someone read the text and passage in the middle of the page. Then discuss the three questions at the bottom of the page.

> ### Luke 18:10-14 (TLB)
> *(10) Two men went to the Temple to pray. One was a proud, self-righteous Pharisee, and the other a cheating tax collector. (11) The proud Pharisee 'prayed' this prayer: 'Thank God, I am not a sinner like everyone else, especially like that tax collector over there! For I never cheat, I don't commit adultery, (12) I go without food twice a week, and I give God a tenth of everything I earn.' (13) But the corrupt tax collector stood at a distance and dared not even lift his eyes to heaven as he prayed, but beat upon his chest in sorrow, exclaiming, 'God, be merciful to me, a sinner.' (14) I tell you, this sinner, not the Pharisee, returned home forgiven! For the proud shall be humbled, but the humble shall be honored.*

Question 2: The Pharisee in the story was not willing to confess that he was a sinner. He stood in the temple telling God how good he was, compared to other men. He even recited a list of all the things that he didn't do. He compared himself to the tax-collector who was praying at the time. The Pharisee congratulated himself that he was not like other men. He considered himself spiritually superior to other men.

Question 3 and 4: According to this passage the Pharisee did not go home forgiven because he did not humble himself before God and turn away from his sin. Confession for this man was a purely perfunctory thing; it was not genuine.

NOTES FOR PAGE 136 IN STUDENT MANUAL

Discuss the two questions at the top of the page.

Question 1: We know that the corrupt tax collector had faced his sinful condition because he did not have the arrogance to defend himself before God. He simply recognized that he was a sinner and that he did not deserve to come into the presence of God.

Question 2: The tax collector was forgiven because he humbled himself before God. He did not try to give reasons why he had sinned. He sorrowfully acknowledged in a simple and forthright manner that he had sinned. Unlike the Pharisee in the story, the tax collector did not look at others and compare himself to them. Instead, he looked at God and compared himself to Him. When we compare ourselves to other men we can always find those who are worse than we are. It is only when we compare ourselves with God and His standard that we are brought to our knees in recognition that we are terribly sinful in the sight of God.

Summarize or have someone read the text.

Take a few minutes to allow each student to write a prayer of confession to the Lord. After they have finished articulating their prayers on paper, ask them to close their eyes and bow their heads for a few moments of silent prayer. Then encourage any who will to pray their prayer aloud to the Lord.

BEING RELATED TO GOD REQUIRES REPENTANCE AND FAITH

Summarize or have someone read the text at the bottom of the page.

> *Acts 3:19 (NIV)*
> *Repent, then, and turn to God, so that your sins may be wiped out, that times of refreshing may come from the Lord.*

NOTES FOR PAGE 138 IN STUDENT MANUAL

Discuss the two questions at the top of the page.

Question 1: Repentance means to agree with God about your sin. To repent means that, in agreement with God, you want to have your life turned around. You want a new attitude of love for God and hatred for sin. Among other things, repentance is asking God to work in your life in such a way that you begin to hate not only the results of sin, but sin itself.

Summarize the text after the first question.

Question 2: Teachers, with this second question on page 138 you must be very sensitive. Do not force answers, because it could mean that a student who has not truly repented may search for a way to rationalize that he has repented. You want this question to help your students recognize that they have not truly repented, rather than forcing them to defend why they *think* they have. Basically, be careful not to back them into a corner. It is very difficult for kids raised in a Christian home, a Christian environment and a Christian church to admit that they really have little or no desire to obey the gospel. Don't reinforce their desire to rationalize through this question.

On the other hand, don't be overly cautious with what a person in your group may share. He may have genuinely repented of his sins. Anyone who shares with apparent confidence and ease about his desire to quit sinning and live for Christ should be encouraged.

Your students may not be able to express why they think they have repented. Don't be depressed by this fact. Instead, gently but firmly help them to understand their need to repent and come into a genuine relationship with Jesus Christ.

Summarize the text and read the Scripture passage in the center of page 138. Then discuss the question that follows.

> ***John 1:12 (NIV)***
> *Yet to all who received him, to those who believed in his name, he gave the right to become children of God.*

Question 3: Receiving Christ is excellently illustrated in the picture on page 139. God the Father gives the gift, Jesus Christ is the gift and the girl represents us. God is giving us the gift of His Son. We must receive Him into our lives.

Summarize the text at the bottom. This text further explains what it means to "receive" Christ.

NOTES FOR PAGE 140 IN STUDENT MANUAL

Discuss the question at the top of the page.

Question 1: The paragraph beneath is very helpful in answering the questions. Students need to know that true, Christian belief involves a willingness to obey God according to the teachings of the Bible. Anyone who says that they believe in Christ, but does not seek to know Him by reading, studying and obeying His word is lying. Worse, they are deceiving themselves. John makes this very clear in 1 John 2:3-6 when he says, "We know that we have come to know him if we obey his commands. The man who says, 'I know him,' but does not do what he commands is a liar, and the truth is not in him. But if anyone obeys his word, God's love is truly made complete in him. This is how we know we are in him: Whoever claims to live in him must walk as Jesus did" (NIV).

Have someone read the Scripture verse in the box in the middle of the page.

> **Romans 10:9 (NIV)**
> *That if you confess with your mouth, "Jesus is Lord," and believe in your heart that God raised him from the dead, you will be saved.*

Take a few minutes to allow your students to answer the questions by checking the boxes at the bottom of the page. Encourage them to be as honest as possible. Ask them not to check a "Yes" answer unless they are sure of their answer. If they do check "No" boxes, encourage them to talk with you, your pastor, or their parents in order to help them resolve their questions. A student who checks a "No" box may be doing a very courageous thing. In many groups, to check "No" beside any one of these questions is an invitation to ostracism by the rest of the group. Be very sensitive. Often a person who is willing to check "No" is saying that he really wants to know the truth. Gentleness and sensitivity, rather than harshness and rebuke, may be all he needs to see that the Gospel is true and that following Christ is the only viable option available to man.

NOTES FOR PAGE 141 IN STUDENT MANUAL

Conclude this study by summarizing the text and reading the Scripture passage from Matthew 11:28-30.

> **Matthew 11:28-30 (TLB)**
> *Come to me and I will give you rest — all of you who work so hard beneath a heavy yoke. Wear my yoke — for it fits perfectly — and let me teach you; for I am gentle and humble, and you shall find rest for your souls; for I give you only light burdens.*

LESSON 13
REVIEW

LESSON OBJECTIVE:

The purpose of this lesson is to have each student articulate clearly what he has learned in this series of lessons by applying his knowledge to three practical situations.

NOTES FOR THIS LESSON

Have your students turn back to page 35 in their manual. We will use the "FIT GOD INTO A 'HARD ANSWERS' PROJECT" exercise to review the things we have learned in this series.

During the first part of this lesson, divide your group into small groups again. Give them about 15 minutes to look through the manual and come up with answers they would give to someone who might be considering suicide.

This exercise should be extremely helpful this time. If you recall, the first time we did this exercise, we were trying to show your students just how little they actually knew about Christianity. By now, they should have a much better understanding of the Christian message, and should, therefore, be able to give much more definitive answers regarding what it means to believe in Jesus Christ. They should also be able to articulate in a much clearer way exactly what God has done for us in Christ Jesus.

After each group has completed the three situations that make up the project on pages 35 and 37, you should lead them in a discussion that will allow them to share with the group what they have decided would be important to tell someone who was giving in to despair.

Use this time to gently correct (or allow the group to correct) any glaring misconceptions about who Jesus Christ is and what He has done for us.

[NOTE: There is probably not enough room under each situation on pages 35 and 37 to adequately answer the questions. We suggest that you have your students turn to the blank page and the inside back cover at the end of the book. This should give them plenty of room to write down their answers.]

Close the discussion by asking them to share anything else they have learned that has helped them in their walk with Christ or which may have increased their desire to further investigate the claims of Christianity.

At the end of this lesson, ask each student to write a prayer thanking God for what He did by giving us His Son. After they have had a few minutes to write, ask them to bow in prayer. Encourage them to offer their prayers to Christ.

Shepherd Ministries
...from Dawson McAllister

1989 ORDER FORM

MANUALS

	STUDENT Price	Code	Qty	TEACHER Price	Code	Qty	TRANSPARENCIES Price	Code	Qty
Student Relationships Volume I	8.75	2010		6.95	2011		43.95	2080	
Student Relationships Volume II	8.75	2012		6.95	2013		43.95	2081	
Student Relationships Volume III	8.75	2014		6.95	2015		43.95	2082	
A Walk With Christ to the Cross	8.95	2030		5.95	2031		24.95	2085	
Through the Resurrection	8.95	2032							
Student Discipleship Volume I	8.50	2020							
Student Discipleship Volume II	8.50	2022							
Who are you, Jesus?	7.95	2040		5.95	2041				
Who is Your God?	7.95	2050							
You, God, and Your Sexuality	3.95	2060							
Preparing Your Teenager for Sexuality (For Parents)	6.95	2065							
Handbook of Financial Faithfulness	6.95	8010							
Dawson Speaks Out on Self Esteem & Loneliness	3.95	2070							

Mail completed order blank to:
SHEPHERD MINISTRIES
2845 W. Airport Frwy. Suite 137
Irving, TX 75062
(214) 570-7599

VIDEOS

	PURCHASE Price	Code	Qty
A Walk with Christ to the Cross	189.95	4120	
When Tragedy Strikes	79.95	4740	
Dawson Speaks Out on Self Esteem and Loneliness	169.95	4050	
Christianity in Overalls (4 Part)	169.95	4020	
Straight Talk About Friends and Peer Pressure (5 Part)	169.95	4040	
Student Workbooks (Set of 5)	6.25	4340	

VIDEOS

	PURCHASE Price	Code	Qty
How to Get Along With Your Parents (4 Sessions)	169.95	4030	
Student Workbooks (Set of 5)	9.75	4330	
Papa, Please Love Me!	169.95	4060	
Tough Questions About Sex	59.95	4010	
Too Young to Die	69.95	4750	
Making Peace with Dad	69.95	4730	
Kids in Crisis	69.95	4720	

SHIP TO:

Name

Organization

Position

Address

City _____ State _____ Zip

Phone ( )

Total order _____

Shipping _____

Total due _____

☐ Please bill me
☐ Payment enclosed

For postage & handling: Add 8% of the total amt.; minimum charge – $2.00. For orders over $150.00, please add 5% of the total amt. For special RUSH shipments (2-day UPS or First Class), add 13% of the total; minimum charge – $4.00.